L.A. 13-8-16

a Marielle
con effetto ... italiano
DOC

francer

# UNKNOWN TUSCANY

# PATRICK ALT

# UNKNOWN TUSCANY

INTRODUCTION

BY

LYLE REXER

MAMMOTH
PLATE PRESS

DEDICATED TO
THE MEMORY OF
MY PARENTS

*I*N THE YEARS I HAVE TRAVELED WITH MY LARGE FORMAT VIEW CAMERAS, I HAVE COME TO BYPASS THE GRAND LANDSCAPE, THE PRETTY SCENE, THE EXPECTED. I FIND MYSELF SEARCHING FOR THOSE THINGS HIDDEN IN PLAIN SIGHT THAT DEFINE AND REVEAL A PLACE. MY EARLIER PHOTOGRAPHS OF UNTRAMMELED NATURE HAVE GIVEN WAY TO THE MARKS PEOPLE LEAVE ON THE LANDSCAPE: THEIR FARMS, THEIR BUILDINGS, AND THEIR SANCTUARIES. NONE OF THOSE PEOPLE ARE IN THESE PICTURES, ONLY WHAT THEY HAVE LEFT BEHIND. A DOORWAY WORN BY TIME, LEAVING TRACES OF ALL WHO HAVE PASSED THROUGH. A VIEW OF AN ANCIENT HILL TOWN BRISTLING WITH AN ARRAY OF SATELLITE DISHES. THE FEMININE FIGURE OF A STONE STATUE, OBLIVIOUS TO THE WATER GENTLY SPLASHING AT HER FEET.

BUT MOSTLY I AM INTERESTED IN STORIES, THE STORIES THAT PROPEL EVERYDAY LIVES, THOSE EVENTS BOTH FASCINATING AND BANAL. WHILE WALKING THROUGH A GARDEN OF AN EIGHTEENTH CENTURY VILLA, I WONDER WHO WAS SITTING IN A GROUPING OF CANE CHAIRS. WAS THEIR CONVERSATION AS SIMPLE AS THE REMINISCENCES OF OLD FRIENDS SHARING CHILDHOOD MEMORIES OR AS MOMENTOUS AS DISCUSSING THE DETAILS OF AN UPCOMING WEDDING? OR WERE THEY TOURISTS EXHAUSTED FROM THE TRAVELS OF THE DAY, RELAXING IN THE COOL OF THE LATE AFTERNOON? AS I STAND ON THE RUBBLE OF A COLLAPSED ROOF TO PHOTOGRAPH AN OLD SHUTTERED WINDOW NEXT TO A MASSIVE STONE SINK, I ASK MYSELF, WHAT FAMILY ONCE OCCUPIED THIS ABANDONED HOUSE? CLUES STILL REMAINING IN ROOMS OF FADED PASTEL COLORS SUGGEST THEY LEFT TO ESCAPE THE VIOLENCE OF THE SECOND WORLD WAR. WHERE DID THEY GO AND WHY DID THEY NOT RETURN TO RECLAIM SUCH A GRAND RESIDENCE? AND HOW IN THE WORLD DID A JET AIRLINER END UP BEHIND A TUSCAN FARMHOUSE?

ONE OF THE REALITIES OF WORKING WITH LARGE VIEW CAMERAS IS THE TIME AND PHYSICAL EFFORT IT TAKES TO SET UP THE EQUIPMENT. THIS MAKES YOU SLOW DOWN AND REALLY OBSERVE WHAT IS IN FRONT OF YOU. THE TAKING OF MARGINAL OR UNINTERESTING IMAGES IS OFTEN ADVERTED BY SPENDING SUCH TIME LOOKING. EACH SHOT THEN BECOMES VERY CAREFULLY CONSIDERED. IN TRAVELING AND EXPLORING TUSCANY BY CAR AND EVEN ON FOOT, I SEARCHED CONTINUOUSLY FOR THOSE SPECIAL COMBINATIONS OF LIGHT AND SUBJECT MATTER WORTHY OF THAT EFFORT. SINCE THE IMAGES WERE ALL TO BE RENDERED IN PLATINUM, ONE OF THE MOST BEAUTIFUL OF PHOTOGRAPHIC PROCESSES, EACH PICTURE HAD TO WORK

WITH ITS SUBTLE AND LONG CONTRAST RANGE AS WELL. AND FINALLY, AND MOST IMPORTANTLY, WHAT I SAW IN FRONT OF ME HAD TO AFFECT ME EMOTIONALLY. WHEN ALL OF THE NECESSARY ELEMENTS WERE IN PLACE, IT WAS TIME TO SET UP THE CAMERA. THE MYRIAD DECISIONS ABOUT CAMERA PLACEMENT, LENS CHOICE, FRAMING THE IMAGE ON THE GROUND GLASS, AND EXPOSURE TIMES ARE THEN MADE. SOMETIMES THE EXPOSURES WERE TAKEN WITH BREATHLESS RAPIDITY TO CAPTURE A CERTAIN LIGHT OR A FURTIVE CAT UNSURE AS TO WHETHER TO HAVE HIS PICTURE TAKEN BY THIS STRANGE APPARITION THAT WAS ME WITH MY CAMERA. AT OTHER TIMES, I WAITED FOR MANY MINUTES FOR A RELUCTANT CLOUD TO DRIFT OVER TO COMPLETE THE DESIRED COMPOSITION.

IT WAS WHILE WAITING FOR THOSE SPECIAL MOMENTS TO TRIP THE SHUTTER THAT I BECAME CONSCIOUS OF ALL MY OTHER SENSES AS WELL, ESPECIALLY THE SOUNDS AND SMELLS AROUND ME, BOTH SUBTLE AND DISTINCT. I HEARD THE BUZZ OF BEES WORKING OVER A FIELD OF YELLOW WILDFLOWERS. THE VERY AIR VIBRATED IN TUNE WITH THE BEATING OF THEIR DELICATE WINGS. THERE WAS THE SOUND OF A GENTLE WIND, RICH WITH THE SMELLS OF THIS ANCIENT LAND, RUSTLING THE LEAVES OF BOTH POPLAR TREES AND GRAPEVINES, EACH WITH ITS OWN INDIVIDUAL AND COMPLEX CHARACTER. I FELT THE MOISTURE IN THE COOL AIR AFTER A BRIEF RAINSTORM, THE LIGHT FROM THE DEPARTING STORM CLOUDS TURNING THE AIR GOLDEN. THEN THERE WAS THE SOFT AND AMIABLE MOOING OF ITALIAN COWS WAITING FOR THEIR PORTRAIT TO BE TAKEN. AS I LOOK OVER ALL OF THE IMAGES IN THIS BOOK, THESE DIVERSE SENSATIONS, VISUAL, AUDITORY, AND AROMATIC, ARE LOCKED IN MY MEMORY OF THE MAKING OF EACH ONE OF THEM.

WHILE YOU VIEW THESE PHOTOGRAPHS, IT IS MY HOPE THAT PERHAPS AN ECHO FROM THESE SENSATIONS WILL EMANATE FROM THE PICTURES AND YOU, TOO, WILL EXPERIENCE SOMETHING OF THE RICH AND ASTOUNDING BEAUTY OF THIS MAGICAL PLACE CALLED TUSCANY.

PATRICK ALT

CULVER CITY, CA

*I*N THE OPENING OF ANDREI TARKOVSKY'S FILM *NOSTALGHIA*, WE SEE A CAR DRIVING BACK AND FORTH ACROSS AN OPEN FIELD IN TUSCANY, A PICTURE POSTCARD SETTING OF ROLLING HILLS AND FIELDS. AND WE HEAR THE NARRATOR SAY, "I'M SICK TO DEATH OF BEAUTIFUL LANDSCAPES." SO BEGINS THE SEARCH FOR SOMETHING DEEPER AND MORE NOURISHING THAN THE MERELY VISIBLE, AN EXPERIENCE BEYOND THE QUOTATION MARKS OF CLICHÉ.

SOMETHING LIKE THIS IMPULSE GUIDED PATRICK ALT ACROSS TUSCANY. ALTHOUGH ALT HAD NEVER BEEN TO ITALY, HE KNEW WHAT HE DIDN'T WANT TO PHOTOGRAPH: THE HILL TOWNS IN SUNLIGHT, THE TABLES LADEN WITH WINE AND FRESH BREAD, THE TERRAZZO VIEWS OF SAN GIMIGNANO AND ITS TOWERS. AND HE KNEW HOW HE DIDN'T WANT TO PHOTOGRAPH: IN LIVING COLOR, MAKING SURE TO GET THE DUSTY BROWNS OF THE FIELDS AND THE RED ROOFS OF THE FARMHOUSES. HE CARRIED HIS 8 X 10 VIEW CAMERA AND HIS COMMITMENT TO AN AESTHETIC OF BLACK, WHITE, AND SHADES OF GRAY. HIS ITALY, PRINTED IN PLATINUM, CELEBRATES A PLACE SHORN OF MEMORIES AND EASY SENTIMENT, A PARALLEL ITALY.

ALT LOOKED WHERE TOURISTS SELDOM DO, IN PARTS OF NORTHERN TUSCANY, FROM LUCCA TO THE APENNINES, WHERE THE FORESTS STILL ENCROACH ON THE VILLAS, WHERE DARKNESS HAS A HOME IN THE BRIGHT TUSCAN LIGHT, WHERE A CERTAIN FORLORN SILENCE INVESTS SMALL TOWNS. ALTHOUGH I HAVE SPENT MUCH TIME IN TUSCANY, ALT VISITED SEVERAL PLACES THAT I HAD NEVER HEARD OF AND OTHERS I HAD LONG WANTED TO SEE BUT NEVER HAVE. THERE WERE PLACES YOU MIGHT PASS THROUGH WITHOUT NOTICING, LIKE GALLUZO, AND OTHERS, LIKE VALLAMBROSA, WHERE ALT AND HIS CAMERA FOUND STRIKING THINGS YOU AND I WOULD PROBABLY MISS WITH OUR COLOR-CLOUDED EYES.

FOR THE MOST PART, ALT AVOIDS THE LONG ESTABLISHING SHOT, THE OPEN VISTA, IN FAVOR OF INTIMATE ENCOUNTERS WITH SPECIFIC FEATURES. HIS TRAVELOGUE IS PRIMARILY AN ITINERARY OF DETAILS: FENCE POSTS, DOORWAYS, BALUSTRADES, STEPS, BENCHES, WALLS, AND FOUNTAINS. THE ANGLE HE TAKES IS NOT THE CLOSE-UP, BUT RATHER THE MIDDLE DISTANCE, AS HE ENCOUNTERS THEM. SO WE NEVER FEEL THE KIND OF CLAUSTROPHOBIA THAT USUALLY MAKES US GLANCE OVER SUCH IMAGES AND WANT TO GET ON TO THE REAL VIEWS. THESE *ARE* THE REAL VIEWS, THE UNKNOWN TUSCANY THAT HIDES IN PLAIN SIGHT.

NEVERTHELESS, I CAN IMAGINE READERS ASKING THEMSELVES ABOUT SOME OF THE IMAGES, WHY THESE? THEY SEEM SO STRAIGHTFORWARD—WHAT WAS HE LOOKING FOR? PEOPLE WHO HAVE BEEN TO ITALY WANT SOMETHING VERY SPECIFIC

FROM PHOTOGRAPHS: AN AID TO RECOLLECTION. THEY SEEK WHAT THEY HAVE ALREADY SEEN, SO THAT THEY CAN EXPERIENCE THE SAME DISCOVERIES OVER AND OVER AGAIN. I AM CERTAIN MOST OF THEM WILL NOT HAVE HAD THE EXPERIENCE THESE PHOTOGRAPHS EXPLORE. THOSE WHO HAVEN'T BEEN THERE SEEK AN IMAGE OF WHAT IS ALREADY KNOWN, THE ITALY THEY WOULD LIKE TO SEE, THE ONE THEY ALREADY KNOW, BUT ONLY IN PICTURES. LIKE TARKOVSKY, ALT IS NOT IN THE NOSTALGIA BUSINESS, NOR IS HE A REPRESENTATIVE OF THE ITALIAN TOURIST INDUSTRY.

WHAT HE IS, HOWEVER, IS AN ARTIST, WHO SEES TUSCANY THROUGH THE MEDIUM OF THE LARGE-FORMAT CAMERA AND THE PLATINUM PRINT. READERS MUST GET USED TO THE IDEA THAT THESE IMAGES EXIST NOT FOR THE SAKE OF ITALY BUT FOR THE SAKE OF THE MEDIUM AND ITS REMARKABLE AESTHETIC PROPERTIES. FOR EXAMPLE, THE VIEW CAMERA, WITH ITS LARGE FORMAT NEGATIVE (AND INFLEXIBLE LENS SYSTEM—NO ZOOM) IS CAPABLE OF REGISTERING OUTSTANDING DETAIL, BOTH CLOSE UP AND IN DEPTH. ALT UNITES THIS CAPABILITY WITH THE TONAL TEXTURE OF PLATINUM (AS OPPOSED TO SILVER) PRINTS AND EXPLOITS THE COMBINATION IN SO MANY WAYS THAT THE FIRST QUESTION ONE NEEDS TO ASK OF AN IMAGE IS NOT WHAT'S IN IT, BUT HOW DOES IT LOOK. THE GRAPE LEAVES OF GREZZANO LOOK AS THOUGH THEY WERE ACTUALLY GRAVEN BY A SCULPTOR, AND THE DULL SURFACE OF THE GRAPE SKINS IS ALMOST PALPABLE. AT FIRST GLANCE, THE IMAGE OF A CHAPEL AND WHEAT FIELD NEAR CORTONA DOES SEEM A BIT LIKE A CONVENTIONAL TUSCAN LANDSCAPE, BUT THE CLARITY OF THE WHEAT GIVES THE IMAGE ANOTHER CENTER OF ATTENTION, NOT THE PICTURESQUE PAST OF HISTORY BUT THE SEASONAL PRESENT (WHICH IS ALSO CYCLICAL). AND PERHAPS MORE: ALT MADE SEVERAL STOPS IN PLACES THAT SAW FIERCE FIGHTING IN WORLD WAR II, AND I CANNOT SHAKE THE SENSE OF ANOTHER TUSCANY, NEARLY FORGOTTEN RATHER THAN UNKNOWN, THE TUSCANY OF FIELDS UNDER WHICH LIE THE MANY DEAD OF A GENERATION THAT IS ABOUT TO PASS FOR GOOD.

IN THIS MEDIUM, WE GIVE UP TEMPORARY PLEASURE FOR MORE ENDURING REVELATION. MOST TRAVELERS WHO HAVE BEEN TO ITALY THINK OF THE TUSCAN LIGHT AS RICHLY COLORED, REDDISH GOLD, OR, AT NOON, BLUE. THE PLATINUM PRINT GIVES A COMPLETELY UNEXPECTED TRANSLATION OF THAT LIGHT, A LIGHT FAR STARKER AND MORE DRAMATIC ON THE ONE HAND, AND SUBTLER ON THE OTHER. I AM THINKING OF ALT'S VIEW OF DUDDA'S GRAPEVINED HILLS AND CLOUDS, ALSO THE IMAGE OF TORRI'S TOPIARY TREES WITH THEIR STARK SHADOWS, AND THE STORM CLOUDS ABOVE THE POPLARS AT IL CORNIOLO. AT THE END OF THE SUMMER, THE WEATHER IN TUSCANY CAN TURN VIOLENT AND STORMY, AND ALT'S CLOUDY SKIES GIVE US GLIMPSES OF THAT POWER. ON THE OTHER HAND, ALT'S POND AT VALLAMBROSA, WITH ITS BLURRED REFLECTIONS, IS A DELICATE CANVAS. VALLAMBROSA WAS A BENEDICTINE MONASTIC CENTER IN THE MIDDLE AGES, AND THE IMAGE SUGGESTS THAT THE REAL MIRACLE STILL MANIFESTS ITSELF, RIGHT IN THE CENTER OF TOWN, IN THE WATER'S TEXTURES—AGAIN, HIDDEN IN PLAIN SIGHT UNTIL THE ARTIST COAXES IT OUT.

THE MENTION OF POPLARS BRINGS UP ANOTHER POINT ABOUT ALT'S UNCONVENTIONAL APPROACH TO TUSCANY. ONE OF HIS MOST SUCCESSFUL IMAGES IS A STATELY YET DELICATE STAND OF POPLARS NEAR SAN GALGANO. WITH ITS RUINED ABBEY AND BEAUTIFUL NATURAL SETTING, SAN GALGANO IS ONE OF THE MOST PHOTOGRAPHED SITES IN SOUTHERN TUSCANY, A REGION ALT MOSTLY AVOIDED. IT IS A MYSTICAL LANDSCAPE THAT FIGURES PROMINENTLY IN THE TARKOVSKY FILM I MENTIONED. ALT DOES THE ABBEY—HOW COULD HE IGNORE IT? BUT HE CAPTURES IT FORMALLY, ABSTRACTLY, AS SERIES OF RECEDING ARCHES. IN ANOTHER IMAGE, HE FINDS, OF ALL THINGS, A PALM TREE GROWING NEXT TO ONE OF ITS WALLS. WE KNOW OF PALM TREES IN THE PIAZZA DE SPAGNA IN ROME, BUT IN TUSCANY? AND AS FOR MYSTICISM, THE POPLAR GROVE IS A MEDITATIONAL INSTRUMENT. ALT HAS PLACED HIS CAMERA TO GIVE US NOT ONLY A SENSE OF THE GROVE'S PERFECT REGULARITY, BUT ALSO SIMULTANEOUS VIEWS DOWN TWO ALLEYS OF TREES AT EITHER EDGE OF THE FRAME, LEADING TO TWO DARK PATHS. THIS SUGGESTS A REFERENCE TO THE POET DANTE, FINDING HIMSELF IN A DARK WOOD "WHEN THE STRAIGHT WAY WAS LOST" AND BEGINNING THE JOURNEY THAT WOULD RESULT IN *THE DIVINE COMEDY*. WHICH PATH? ALT SEEMS TO ASK.

I HAVE BEEN TRYING TO GET AT THE QUALITIES OF PARTICULAR IMAGES AS A WAY OF POINTING OUT WHY ALT'S TUSCANY IS SO UNUSUAL, BUT REALLY THE SENSE OF PLACE HE EVOKES IS SOMETHING MORE ELUSIVE. IT MAY BE JUST THAT TRICK OF FORCING US TO SUPPLY THE COLOR OF TUSCANY, IMAGINATIVELY, OF GIVING US THE POETRY OF UNDERSTATEMENT. ONE OF THE PLACES ALT CLEARLY FOUND MOST FASCINATING WAS THE GIARDINO GRAZZONI AT COLLODI. WITH ITS ELABORATE, TERRACED GARDENS AND OVER-THE-TOP SCULPTURAL DECORATIONS, THE GARDEN EMBODIES A FANTASY MADE REAL. ALT TURNS IT BACK INTO A VISION, A STATIC WAKING DREAM. HE REASSERTS THE POWER OF ART OVER EVERYDAY REALITY, NO MATTER HOW PICTURESQUE, A POWER TO TRANSFORM THE REALITY OF THE TOURIST AND VISITOR. FOR ALT IS NOT INTERESTED IN BRINGING BACK IMAGES OF SOMETHING ALREADY THERE AND WAITING FOR US, BUT RATHER IN CAPTURING IMAGES OF A TUSCANY THAT DOES NOT YET EXIST, THAT COMES INTO BEING ONLY AS HE DEVELOPS HIS PICTURES. THIS IS THE UNKNOWN TUSCANY, NOT OF UNTRAVELED BYWAYS, NOT OF UNEXPECTED LIGHT AND SHADOW, BUT OF THE ARTIST'S IMAGINATION.

LYLE REXER

BROOKLYN, NEW YORK

# PLATES

8

9

20

26

28

38

# PLATES

Wooden Gate
and Stairs,
Chiesa la
Certosa di
Firenze–
Galluzo

1

Civitella
with Cat

2

Sculpted
Trees
and
Building–
Torri

3

Tree-Lined
Road–Outside
Alberese

4

Doorway and
Windows,
Abandoned
Barn–
Il Corniolo

5

Bridge and
Bell Tower–
Camaggione

6

Ponte di
Medici–
Pontasieve

7

Mosaic Wall and
Stairs, Giardino
Garzoni–
Collodi

8

Sculpture and
Fountain with
Stone Steps,
Palagio
Fiorentino–
Stia

9

View of
Church
through
Olive Trees–
San
Gimingnano

10

Door and
Windows–
Barco

11

View through
Cypress–
Outside Asciano

12

Metal Cross
and Arches–
Sant' Agata

13

After the Rain,
Ava Maria
Shrine–
La Maesta,
Alta Mugello

14

Palm Tree–
San Galgano

15

Neoclassic
Church—
Forsini

16

Torso and
Fountain—
Palagio
Fiorentino,
Stia

17

Pasture with
Horses—
Casanova

18

Vineyard and
Church—
Casciano

19

Cane Chairs
and Sculpture,
Villa Manci—
Segromigno

20

Airliner on
Hill—
Roccastrada

21

Brick Building
and Trees—
San Galgano

22

Field of
Wildflowers
and Abandoned
House—Outside
Asciano

23

Sculpture
and Villa,
Giardino
Grazoni—
Collodi

24

Stairways,
Giardino
Grazoni—
Collodi

25

Door and
Windows—
Barco

26

Stone Table
with Fallen
Leaves, Palagio
Fiorentino—
Stia

27

Fountain at
Night—
Cortona

28

Stone
Fountain—
Forsini

29

View
of San
Gimingnano
with Cloud

30

Front of
Rectory—
Civitella

31

 STREET SCENE
AFTER RAIN–
LONDA
32

 BRANCHES AND
WATERFALL–
BAGNI DI LUCCA
33

 DOUBLE ARCH
AND WOOD
RAILING,
TERME TAMERICI–
MONTECATINI
34

 CHAPEL FAÇADE,
CHIESA LA
CERTOSA DI
FIRENZE–
GALLUZO
35

 TUSCAN
LANDSCAPE–
DIPTYCH (L)
36

 TUSCAN
LANDSCAPE–
DIPTYCH (R)
37

 PONTE DI
DIAVOLO–
BAGNI DI LUCCA
38

 AQUADUCT
AND TOWER–
LUCCA
39

 SCULPTURE AND
BALLISTRADE,
VILLA MANCI–
SEGROMIGNO
40

 CURVING BRIDGE
AND CHAPEL–
IL CORNIOLO
41

 IRON GATE AND
STONE POST–
FORSINI
42

 SYCAMORE,
TERME TAMERICI–
MONTECATINI
43

 STONE WALL
WITH ROSES–
FORSINI
44

 CHIANTI GRAPES
AND ROAD–
DUDDA
45

 GOTHIC ARCHES–
SAN GALGANO
46

SHUTTERED
WINDOW AND
VINES–
ABANDONED
FARMHOUSE
OUTSIDE ASCIANO
47

OLD TRAIN
AND TRACKS–
STIA

48

ALLIED WAR
MEMORIAL–
AREZZO

49

CHAPEL AND
WHEAT FIELD–
TORRI

50

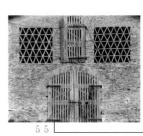

VIEW OUTSIDE
PIENZA

51

DISTANT
BUILDINGS,
SUNSET–
CORTONA

52

VIEW OF SANTA
BIAGNO AND
MONTEPULCIANO

53

POND–
VALLAMBROSA

54

BARN DOOR,
MONSIGNOR
DELLA CASA–
IL CORNIOLO

55

ROADSIDE BENCH
AND TREES–
LA MAESTA,
ALTO MUGELLO

56

POPLAR GROVE–
SAN GALGANO

57

OLIVE GROVE
TERRACES–
CASTELLO DI
MONTECCHIO

58

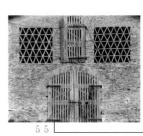

ARCHES,
TERME DI
MONTECATINI–
MONTECATINI

59

THE GOD
PAN AND
BALLISTRADE,
GIARDINO
GRAZONI–
COLLODI

60

THE CHAPEL AT
LA MOCHETA–
ALTO MUGELLO

61

GRAPE VINES
AND ABANDONED
BUILDING–
VESPIGNANO

62

CHIANTI
GRAPES–
GREZZANO

63

FIELD OF
FLOWERS AND
THE HERMITAGE–
SAN GALGANO

64

VIEW OF CUNA
WITH TREE

65

TREE-LINED
ROAD OUTSIDE
ALBERESE

66

ENTRANCE TO
TERME
MONTACATINI–
MONTACATINI

67

POPLAR GROVE
AND CLEARING
STORM–
IL CORNIOLO

68

ROLLING HILLS,
SUNSET–
OUTSIDE PIENZA

69

VILLA AND
CLOUDS–
MUGNANO

70

VIEW OF
ASCIANO WITH
AQUADUCT

71

VIEW OF
RIFREDO

72

COWS AND ROAD–
CUNA

73

SCULPTURE AND
FOUNTAIN WITH
BANANA LEAVES,
VILLA MANCI–
SEROMIGNO

74

# ACKNOWLEDGMENTS

First and foremost, I wish to thank Susan Spiritus, my dealer and dearest friend for almost three decades. Her unstinting hard work and belief in me has allowed me the opportunity to evolve and grow as an artist, a luxury most rare and greatly appreciated. Without her, this project would never have happened. My agent and editor, Suzanne G. Fox of Red Bird Publishing, walked me through the complexities of book publishing with professionalism and humor. She was the keystone to this whole project. To Brad Fleming of Hemlock Printers, whose hard work made this book the beautiful object it is and whose function as the West Coast's most perfect straight man made this project a joy as well. Mary Lou Kelpe translated my design ideas into a cohesive whole and was an integral element in the final creation of this book. I also wish to thank Lyle Rexer, whose kind and thoughtful introduction helped illuminate the beauty that is Italy and my works related to it. To my sister-in-law, Peggy Rottner, whose generosity allowed us to come and be introduced to the Tuscan countryside where amongst the rolling hills and vineyards the seed of this project was planted. To my parents, John and Peggy Alt, whose passing provided me the funding to do this book, but sadly who will never be able to see it finished. And finally to my wife Melissa, the love of my life and partner in all things. She was by my side when all of these images were made. Her comments and support have made this project the delight it was while we explored this most extraordinary place together. These photographs are a personal record of our journey.

# TECHNICAL NOTES

THE PICTORIALISTS, A GROUP OF PHOTOGRAPHERS ACTIVE BETWEEN THE YEARS 1880 TO 1920, WORKED USING THE PLATINUM PROCESS EXTENSIVELY BECAUSE OF ITS DELICACY OF TONAL RANGES AND ITS POTENTIAL FOR EXPRESSING THE CHARACTERISTICS OF MORE TRADITIONAL ART-MAKING METHODS SUCH AS DRAWING AND ETCHING. CHAMPIONED BY ALFRED STEIGLITZ AND THE PHOTO SECESSION, PLATINUM WAS USED BY ALMOST ALL OF THE GREAT PHOTOGRAPHERS DURING THIS TIME, INCLUDING EDWARD WESTON, EDWARD STEICHEN, AND IMOGEN CUNNINGHAM. PLATINUM PRINTS HAVE BEEN REFERRED TO AS THE QUINTESSENTIAL BLACK-AND-WHITE PHOTOGRAPH. THE PROCESS STARTED DISAPPEARING DURING WORD WAR I DUE TO THE SOARING PRICES AND SCARCITY OF PLATINUM. THE EARLY 1980S SAW A RENEWED INTEREST IN ALTERNATIVE PROCESSES, WITH PLATINUM BEING ONE OF MANY.

INVENTED IN 1873, PLATINUM PRINTING IS ONE OF THE OLDEST PHOTOGRAPHIC PROCESSES, NOTED FOR ITS SUBTLETY IN RENDERING THE TONALITIES OF THE MIDDLE GRAYS. IT IS THE MOST ARCHIVAL OR LONG LASTING OF ALL PHOTOGRAPHS. IMPERVIOUS TO LIGHT, FADING AND ACID DAMAGE, IT IS CAPABLE OF LASTING 1,000 YEARS WITHOUT CHANGE. PLATINUM PRINTS ARE CONTACT PRINTS – MEANING THE PHOTOGRAPHS ARE THE SIZE OF THE NEGATIVES.

EACH IMAGE IS THE RESULT OF AN INTRICATE SERIES OF STEPS. THE PROCESS BEGINS WITH BLANK SHEETS OF SPECIALIZED PAPER. LIGHT-SENSITIVE IRON SALTS ARE MIXED WITH PLATINUM AND/OR PALLADIUM, A CLOSELY RELATED METAL, IN SOLUTION AND APPLIED EVENLY TO THE PAPER, USING A BRUSH OR GLASS ROD. THE PAPER IS DRIED AND THEN HUMIDIFIED. THE NEGATIVE IS PLACED ON THE DRIED COATED PAPER AND BOTH ARE PUT INTO A CONTACT PRINTING FRAME. TRADITIONALLY THE SUN WAS USED FOR EXPOSURE. NOW ULTRAVIOLET LIGHT SOURCES ARE USED. EXPOSURE TIMES RANGE FROM TWO MINUTES TO TWO HOURS. THE PRINT IS DEVELOPED, USUALLY IN A DEVELOPER HEATED TO OVER 100 DEGREES, CLEARED, WASHED, AND THEN AIR-DRIED.

BECAUSE OF THE NUMBER OF VARIABLES INVOLVED, SUCH AS CHANGES OF HUMIDITY, AGE OF THE CHEMISTRY, PAPER BATCH, AND THE POSITION OF THE MOON, PLATINUM PRINTERS MUST HAVE A GREAT DEAL OF PATIENCE AND FORBEARANCE. FOR THESE REASONS, NO TWO PRINTS ARE EVER EXACTLY ALIKE.

*P*ATRICK ALT HAS BEEN A FINE ART PHOTOGRAPHER FOR THIRTY-FIVE YEARS AND IS CONSIDERED A MASTER OF LARGE FORMAT PHOTOGRAPHY. WORKING WITH CAMERAS AS SMALL AS 8 X 10 TO THE 100-YEAR-OLD 18 X 22 INCH MAMMOTH PLATE CAMERA, HE EXPRESSES IN HIS WORK THE HISTORICAL HIGH REGARD FOR THE FINELY CRAFTED HAND-MADE PRINT. HIS IMAGES OF NUDES, STILL LIFES, AND LANDSCAPES ARE PRINTED IN TONED SILVER, CYANOTYPE, AND PRIMARILY IN THE EXQUISITE ALTERNATIVE PROCESS OF HANDCOATED PLATINUM/PALLADIUM. HIS WORK IS EXHIBITED EXTENSIVELY AND IS IN MANY PRIVATE AND CORPORATE COLLECTIONS.

*L*YLE REXER IS THE AUTHOR OF SEVERAL BOOKS ON ART AND PHOTOGRAPHY. ONE OF HIS RECENT BOOKS IS THE ACCLAIMED *PHOTOGRAPHY'S ANTIQUARIAN AVANT GARDE: THE NEW WAVE IN OLD PROCESSES.* HIS LATEST BOOK IS *HOW TO LOOK AT OUTSIDER ART.* HE HAS PUBLISHED NUMEROUS CATALOG ESSAYS ON CONTEMPORARY ARTISTS AND COLLECTIONS, AND HAS CONTRIBUTED FEATURE-LENGTH ARTICLES TO PUBLICATIONS SUCH AS *THE NEW YORK TIMES, ART IN AMERICA, ART ON PAPER,* AND *APERTURE.* HE ALSO WRITES REGULARLY FOR THE DESIGN MAGAZINE *GRAPHIS.* LYLE RESIDES IN BROOKLYN, NEW YORK.

PHOTO: JERRY SPAGNOLI

Published By
Mammoth Plate Press
8928 Carson St.
Culver City, CA 90232
310-815-1551 Fax: 310-815-1575

www.patrickalt.com

Photographs © 2006 by Patrick Alt
Introduction © 2006 by Lyle Rexer
ISBN:0-9772585-0-5/978-0-9772585-0-5

Book Design by Mary Lou Kelpe and Patrick Alt
Editorial Services by Suzanne G. Fox, Red Bird Publishing
Images Scanned and Printed By Hemlock Printers Ltd., Vancouver, Canada
Bound by Roswell Binding, Phoenix, Arizona
Printed on Mohawk 65# Warm White Vellum Cover

Platinum Photographs from this book may be ordered from:
Susan Spiritus Gallery
3929 Birch
Newport Beach, CA 92660
949-474-4321 Fax: 949-474-4204

PRINTED IN CANADA